Amazing Archaeology

# Ötzi the Iceman

by Julie Murray

Dash!
**LEVELED READERS**
An Imprint of Abdo Zoom • abdobooks.com

### Level 1 – Beginning
Short and simple sentences with familiar words or patterns for children who are beginning to understand how letters and sounds go together.

### Level 2 – Emerging
Longer words and sentences with more complex language patterns for readers who are practicing common words and letter sounds.

### Level 3 – Transitional
More developed language and vocabulary for readers who are becoming more independent.

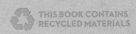

abdobooks.com

Published by Abdo Zoom, a division of ABDO, PO Box 398166, Minneapolis, Minnesota 55439. Copyright © 2022 by Abdo Consulting Group, Inc. International copyrights reserved in all countries. No part of this book may be reproduced in any form without written permission from the publisher. Dash!™ is a trademark and logo of Abdo Zoom.

Printed in the United States of America, North Mankato, Minnesota.
102021
012022

Photo Credits: Alamy, Getty Images, iStock, Science Source, Shutterstock
Production Contributors: Kenny Abdo, Jennie Forsberg, Grace Hansen, John Hansen
Design Contributors: Candice Keimig, Neil Klinepier

**Library of Congress Control Number: 2021940206**

**Publisher's Cataloging in Publication Data**

Names: Murray, Julie, author.
Title: Otzi the Iceman / by Julie Murray
Description: Minneapolis, Minnesota : Abdo Zoom, 2022 | Series: Amazing archaeology | Includes online resources and index.
Identifiers: ISBN 9781098226664 (lib. bdg.) | ISBN 9781644946398 (pbk.) | ISBN 9781098227500 (ebook) | ISBN 9781098227920 (Read-to-Me ebook)
Subjects: LCSH: Otzi (Ice mummy)--Juvenile literature. | Ice mummies--Juvenile literature. | Human remains (Archaeology)--Juvenile literature. | Ice patch archaeology--Juvenile literature. | Excavations (Archaeology)--Juvenile literature. | Archaeology and history--Juvenile literature.
Classification: DDC 937--dc23

# Table of Contents

# Ötzi the Iceman

Ötzi lived more than 5,300 years ago. He is one of the best-preserved **natural mummies** ever found.

In 1991, two hikers discovered Ötzi on a mountain ridge between Austria and Italy. His upper body was sticking out of **glacial ice** at 10,530 feet (3,210 m).

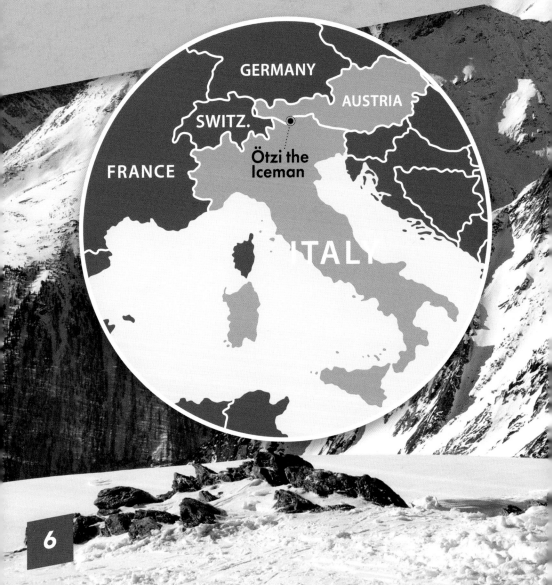

GERMANY

AUSTRIA

SWITZ.

FRANCE

Ötzi the Iceman

ITALY

# Frozen in Time

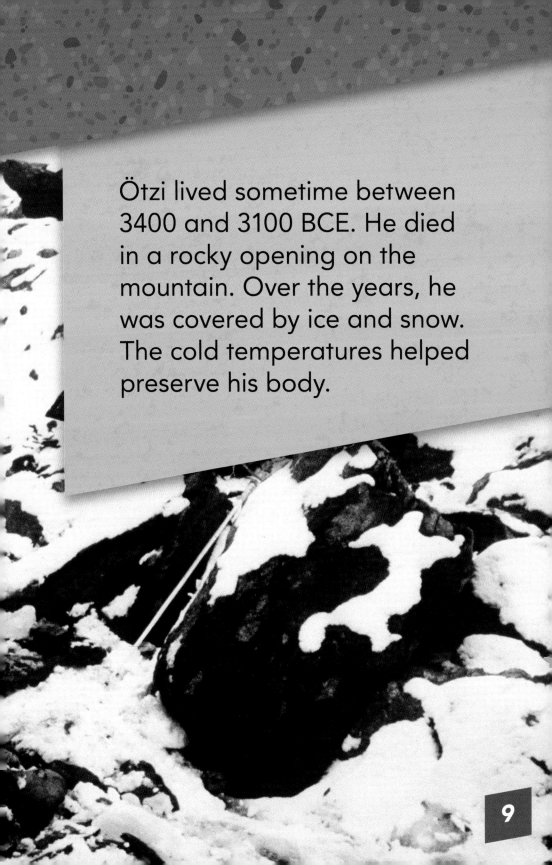

Ötzi lived sometime between 3400 and 3100 BCE. He died in a rocky opening on the mountain. Over the years, he was covered by ice and snow. The cold temperatures helped preserve his body.

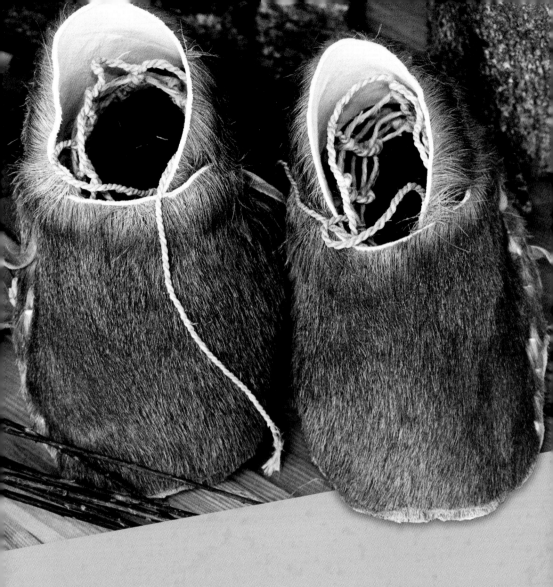

Scientists are not sure who Ötzi was. His things suggest he had not lived with people for some time. He had a bearskin hat and a robe made from different animal skins.

His shoes were made of deer hide and were stuffed with grass. He had a bow and arrows, and a copper axe. A wooden backpack carried his goods and tools.

13

Scans of Ötzi's body revealed an arrowhead lodged in his shoulder. It also showed a wound on his head. These likely led to his death.

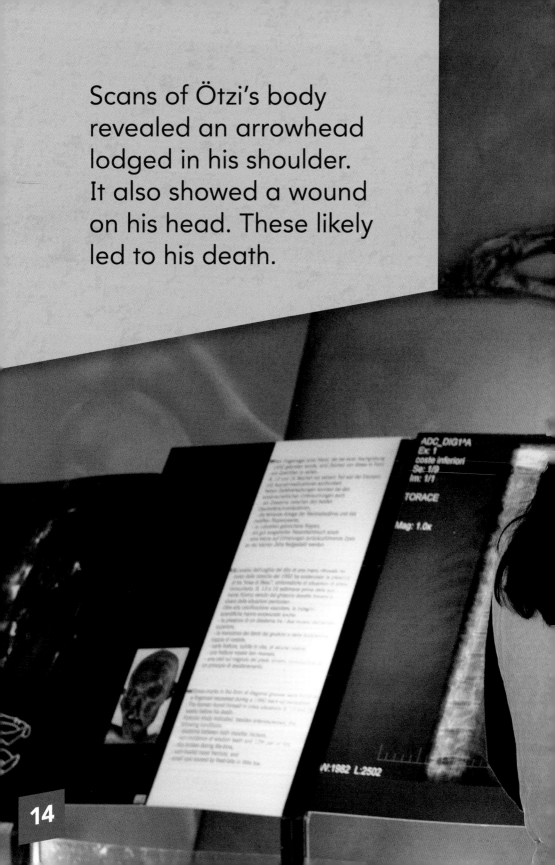

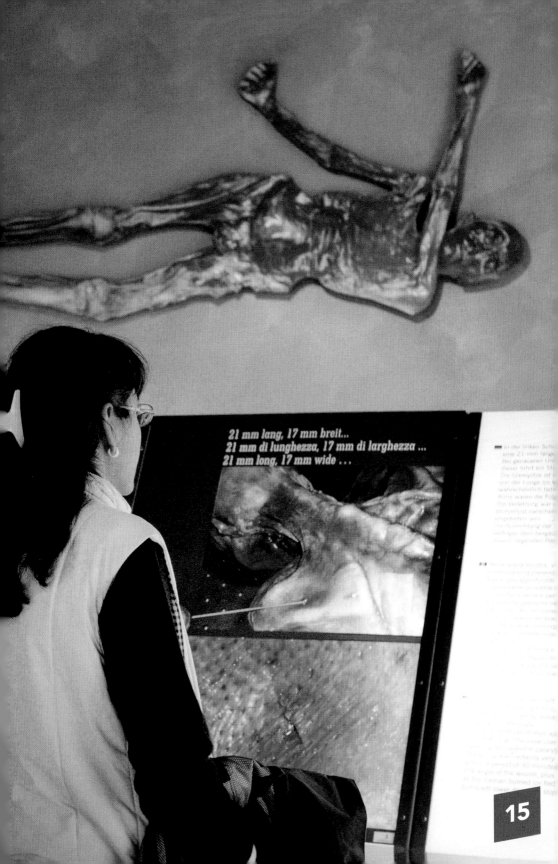

21 mm lang, 17 mm breit...
21 mm di lunghezza, 17 mm di larghezza ...
21 mm long, 17 mm wide . . .

Scientists believe Ötzi was around 45 years old when he died. He was about 5 feet 2 inches tall (1.6 m) and weighed 110 pounds (50 kg). He had longer dark hair, a beard, and brown eyes.

The food in Ötzi's stomach was not digested. This means that he ate soon before he died. His last meal was **ibex** meat, red deer, and grain cereals.

# Ötzi Today

Today, Ötzi and his belongings are on display in the South Tyrol Museum of Archaeology in Bolzano, Italy. A model of him shows what he might have looked like.

# More Facts

- Ötzi was named after the Ötztal Alps. This is where his mummy was found.

- He had 61 tattoos on his body. The tattoos are groups of black lines. They were made using fireplace soot or ash.

- Researchers discovered that Ötzi had broken ribs, **arthritis**, and **Lyme disease**.

# Glossary

**arthritis** – a disease of the joints in which they swell and become painful.

**glacial ice** – thick layers of snow that slowly press down on each other, forming a glacier.

**ibex** – a wild mountain goat with long, thick horns and a beard.

**Lyme disease** – an inflammatory disease caused by bacteria that are transmitted by ticks. Symptoms include rash, headache, fever, and chills.

**natural mummy** – a deceased person or animal whose body and organs were preserved without the introduction of chemicals by humans.

# Index

## Online Resources

**Booklinks**
**NONFICTION NETWORK**
FREE! ONLINE NONFICTION RESOURCES